What Next

A Memoir Toward World Peace

Other Titles by Walter Mosley

FICTION

Six Easy Pieces

Bad Boy Brawley Brown

Gone Fishin'

A Little Yellow Dog

Devil in a Blue Dress

A Red Death

White Butterfly

Black Betty

RL's Dream

Blue Light

Always Outnumbered, Always Outgunned

Walkin' the Dog

Futureland

Fearless Jones

NON FICTION

Workin' on the Chain Gang

Black Genius

What Next

A Memoir Toward World Peace

Walter Mosley

The text of this book is composed in Kernel
Cover design by Lesia Green
Text design by Michelle D. Wright

Library of Congress Cataloging-in-Publication Data

Mosley, Walter.
  What next : a memoir toward world peace / Walter Mosley.--
1st ed.
      p. cm.
  ISBN 1-57478-020-4
 1. United States--Foreign relations--2001---Philosophy. 2.
International relations--Philosophy. 3. African Americans—
Social conditions--1975- 4. African Americans--Race identity.
5. September 11 Terrorist Attacks, 2001--Causes. 6. September
11 Terrorist Attacks, 2001--Influence. 7. Mosley, Walter. 8.
African Americans--Biography.
I. Title.

E895.M67 2003
327.73'009'0511--dc21

                              2002156736

Distributed by Publishers Group West
Printed in the U.S.A.

This book is dedicated to Haki Madhubuti,
poet, educator, activist, father, and man.

America is the architect of globalization, but Americans are not global.

- *Manthia Diawara*

Prefatory Note

Everyone is invited to read this book. But before you begin, you should know that it has been written specifically as an address to African America. It is a reflection on our history and subsequently upon our future—especially with regard to the current war that the United States has entered.

Because of the unique history and daily experiences of African American people, I believe that we have a singular perspective on the qualities of revenge, security, and peace that will positively inform the direction of our nation's sometimes ill-considered stands. It is, I believe, important to air certain ideas and insights that arise from that African American experience as they relate to our enemies and our friends.

Part One

A Father's Story

When I was eight, I asked my father if he was afraid to go off and fight in World War II. He said, "No, honey. I wasn't afraid. You see, I knew that the Germans were fighting the Americans, but I didn't know that *I* was an American."

"Why not?" I asked.

"Nobody thought that Negroes were Americans where I was raised," he said. "We couldn't vote, we had no rights that couldn't be

What Next

taken away by white people, and most of us believed that we weren't really equal to whites. So I thought that the Germans would just pass me by looking for their American enemies."

"Did they?" I asked, and my father laughed. I always loved it when my father laughed. Humor in our house was both strength and knowledge.

"No," he said. "Those Germans wanted to kill me just as much they wanted to kill every other foreign soldier. As a matter of fact, them shooting at me was what made me realize that I really was an American. That's why, when I was discharged, I left the South and came here to Los Angeles. Because I couldn't live among people who didn't know or couldn't accept what I had become in danger and under fire in the war."

My father always taught by telling stories about his experiences. His lessons were about morality and art and what insects and birds and human beings had in common. He told me what it meant to be a man and to be a Black man. He taught me about love and responsibility, about beauty, and how to make gumbo. My father's instructions have sustained me in the complex life we live here in America. Some of his lessons I'm still working out over forty years later.

What did he intend for me to learn when he told me about the war and his safety zone of race? I already knew that I was an American because every Election Day my parents made a big deal about going out to vote. California was our home, and I was so insulated by their love that racism seemed like a far off, almost mythical foe. Maybe this story about the war was just a humorous tale. But no, if you had been there, you would have felt the passion and deep emotion. You would have heard the relief in his laughter.

When I went to school, there were no Black philosophers, at least none that I was aware of, who were recognized by Western universities. All of the philosophers I studied were white (with a few Eastern exceptions), and, for that matter, they were all male. Africa, the cradle of civilization, seemed to have no footing in the highest form of human thought. Even the few philosophers who were obviously born on the Mother

What Next

Continent were most often represented in white face. This is changing somewhat, but I'm still of a generation whose minds' eyes were trained to see white men as the only leaders and scientists and thinkers.

I would have been completely brainwashed by this lopsided and racist view of the world if it weren't for my father. He was a deep thinker and an irrepressible problem solver. He was a Black Socrates, asking why and then spoiling ready-made replies. He laughed when things got really bogged down, but he was no Sophist. My father cared about the world he lived in, and so he admitted his confusion about his place in America because he didn't want me to make the same mistake in my life. Or, if I did make a misstep, he wanted to make sure that I could find the remedy in his great treasury of tales.

The first thing I had to work out was that his story unfolded in three stages: First the fearless ignorance that blinded my father to his real place in the world and the real threat of the war; then the violent and frightening experience that made him see that he had been wrong all those years; and finally the wisdom he gained, which showed him that he had to break away from the world he had known, and the world that knew him, in order to act on the knowledge he had gained. His was a path set out in ideas and a system of thought based on a unique experience.

On the face of it, one might think that my father was just slow. Why didn't he see that if he put on a uniform and crossed the mighty Atlantic that his life would be in jeopardy just like the white soldiers who came from America? This story, you might think, only proves that LeRoy Mosley didn't have the sense to come in out of the rain. But my father had been seeing Black men in uniforms go along almost invisibly his entire life. They were butlers and porters and hotel clerks, red caps and jazz band members who labored in the background, in the shadows of their own skins. There were even Black policemen in my father's time, but they were not allowed to arrest whites. They weren't even allowed in certain parts of the police station. Black men in uniform, for the most part, went unnoticed. But even if some white soldier did see him, why would he worry?

What Next

Racist doctrine held then (as today) that the only true Americans were white Americans. Native Americans, Blacks, Asians, Mexicans, and all other dark-skinned people were, at best, temporary visitors who served in menial posts. They couldn't make demands or see themselves in important roles in American culture. The images on movie screens, in magazines and newspapers, and storefront windows all extolled Euro-Americans. If an Asian or Black were depicted, it was in service or for a joke. There certainly weren't any Black war heroes killing or being killed.

Jesus was a white man, and God was his sire. Taking this as his cue, my father decided that he was not considered a part of the greater moral and political system. White America and white Germany had a problem with each other; and if my father was dressed in a uniform and sent over there, it was only for him to be of service—or a joke.

When he was drafted, my father had to take a battery of tests. These tests revealed his ability to read, work with arithmetic, and type—skills that made him perfect for statistics, which at that time basically meant keeping tallies of the dead. So they gave my father a desk in a tent, a typewriter, a stack of long sheets, and an M1 rifle. Every now and then, orders would come through, and he would have to jump into the back of a truck with these tools, only to be deposited in some new countryside a few miles from the fighting.

The new land, Europe, was strange. Black soldiers weren't treated with the condescension or contempt that was their daily fare in the United States. Many white Europeans conversed with him openly, some thanked him, a few of the ladies even invited him home. My father chalked up these odd experiences to the strange character of Europe. He wondered about these unusual customs, but he didn't question his worldview until the day the Germans broke through Allied lines and marched on his bivouac.

"They were shooting at *me*, Walter," he said. "I could hear their bullets cutting through the air. When I picked up that rifle, I knew that I had just as much on the line as all those white soldiers. And when I thought about it afterwards, I realized that if I had just as much to lose, then I deserved all that any white man deserved. I became an American in France, under fire and afraid for my life."

So my father became an American, and I became a possibility in his life: a son who would be an American from the moment he was born, with all the rights, privileges, and hopes of any other American.

And he wasn't alone in this newfound and ecstatic view of his place in the world. A new wave of racial unrest swept the nation after World War II. The Civil Rights Movement blossomed. Black Americans began to demand their rights. They came out of the shadows and took advantage of the opportunities inherent in a nation that had been taking advantage of them for centuries. The term "American" took on a new face, and there was a resurgence of commitment to the Bill of Rights and the Constitution.

We (people of all hues and persuasions) are the heirs of this political movement. And I, personally, am the beneficiary of my father's interpretation of the structure of his experience. He graduated from the school of hard knocks and passed me his notes, in hopes that I would be able to make the transition, if ever a time came when I found myself in a situation where my perception of the world proved to be wrong. If I survived that realization, just as he survived the German attack, he hoped that I could go back to his words and discover a path of my own.

I Wasn't the Enemy

On the morning of September 11, 2001, I was talking on the phone and looking down on the Hudson River from my southward-facing Greenwich Village apartment window. I heard a concussion, felt it almost. I looked around but saw nothing until my eyes rose up and caught sight of the World Trade Center. The gash on the upper side of the north tower was black and spewing smoke. There was also a trail of smoke down the left side of the building that went all the way to the street.

I was confused about that trail of smoke. I tried to figure out how it fit with the smoking wound. It wasn't until some time later, when the second jetliner crashed into the southern tower, that I understood that downward trail of dark vapor.

That cascading column came to mean to me everything about the war that was forming in peoples' minds around the world. It was a sign that I couldn't read clearly, but still I knew there were deadly ramifications to its manifestation.

I won't belabor the story here. We all went through it: our own planes raining death and destruction down upon our nation's most identifiable and important cities and structures. The towers falling, the heroic struggles, the war being waged upon our one-time allies against the U.S.S.R.—all of this presaged in that dense black column that dissipated within minutes of its inception.

For months after this event, I, like so many Americans, was lost in a kind of anxiety-ridden daze. I worried about world war, about radical religious extremists wresting the reins of power

What Next

from some nation with nuclear capabilities. I worried about air travel and subway cars, about doomsday plagues, and about my nation falling under the sway of fascist rule. There was a deep disquiet in my heart, and I didn't know how to get at it except by worrying about nebulous issues far beyond my immediate control.

This is, of course, how the human mind works. When we feel menaced, we try to protect ourselves by considering every possible threat that might arise. The problem in this case, however, was that there was no defense against falling jetliners, religious hardliners, and the resort to unqualified nationalism.

The thing I feared most was the healing quality that time has on the human heart. I knew that after a while I would fall back into complacency —that I would learn to accept that which I knew was unacceptable.

Then I remembered my father's story.

The structure of this event was similar to his experiences in World War II. There I was talking on the phone, unafraid of the international terrorism that had been in the headlines since Germany had hosted the Olympics. My father's words echoed in my mind: *They weren't fighting me.*

Of course, I was aware of the attack on the WTC eight years earlier. I had later decided against renting an office there because it had been a target earlier on. But I hadn't ever fully realized the threat. I wasn't at war with the factions of the Middle East. If anything, I told myself, it was international capitalism and its obsession with petroleum that was their enemy.

Again, my father's words came to me. *It was the Germans and the Americans who were at war... I didn't know that I was an American.*

There was the blissful ignorance and then the frightening moment when I realized that I was on one side of the conflict, that the men who destroyed those buildings saw me as their enemy, too. All that remained was to figure out what concepts I had to leave behind and what new ideas I needed to nurture.

Portent in a Column of Smoke

I decided to start writing, to see if I could, like my father before me, determine on a path of action that would express, in real terms, my hopes and my convictions in a world gone haywire.

For the first time, I truly appreciated my father's predicament in 1945. His decision to leave Texas was no simple matter. He was ready for a new world. But was the new world ready for him? Could he shuck off the misconceptions of a lifetime and change the terms of discourse? Could he, seemingly a solitary thinker in a place where Negroes were told they couldn't think, express his ideas of equality in a world where he wasn't on equal footing?

Every day for my father was a challenge. When he returned home from the war, most of his good friends among his Black soldier peers were alive and hopeful, but the majority of his old friends in Texas had died. Many of the young Black Texans he had known had passed away from disease and self-inflicted brutality. He realized that he had been safer fighting in the greatest war in the history of the world than he would have been on the streets of the Fifth Ward, Houston, Texas. That became another one of his lessons.

So, he got on a bus and took the long trip to Los Angeles. There, he saw a diner downtown that catered to both whites and Blacks. He smiled and went in to order an ice cream sundae. He felt proud and happy at first, but he was later shocked when the white man sitting next to him suffered a heart attack and died right there in his arms. He realized then that he might have

What Next

escaped the oppression of the South, but there was no escape from mortality.

Armed with these sobering experiences, my father took up his struggle to make a life worth living in a world that had denied his ancestors for centuries. He counted his small victories and laughed at his simple mistakes. He and many of his contemporaries entered a world where they were overmatched, undercut, and lied to day and night by their enemies, their loved ones, and by almost all of those with so-called objective knowledge of the world. They were dismissed by public opinion and excluded from serious avenues of public discourse.

That's the experience of people of color, by and large, in America today.

Thousands of dark people are dying daily in the towns and villages and cities of Africa. We in the United States know this, but it doesn't seem to matter to us any more than a popular television show coming to the end of its run. Millions of people, maybe more than ever in the history of the world, are languishing in slavery and forced labor in the Sudan and Haiti and many other countries. There are even slaves here in the United States, men and women trapped in the modern growth industry of private prisons, not to mention those caught in the traffic of forced prostitution.

Every night on every station there is some sit-com that makes a joke about what happens to young men in prison—but still we do nothing. Not only are these men raped, humiliated, and emotionally shattered, but they become infected with AIDS and Hepatitis-C, diseases that they bring home to our communities. And we, literally, just laugh.

Pol Pot, Osama bin Laden, Noriega, Saddam Hussein, the white South African regimes, Baby Doc, and Papa Doc, and hundreds of other despots, mass murderers, and madmen were bought and paid for, trained and indoctrinated by our dollars to protect the interests of our international industrial complex. War and poverty, disease and hopelessness are ravaging half the world, while the other half wonders how long it will be able to stay out of the maelstrom.

All this is *our* responsibility. Every child wasting

What Next

away under his mother's powerless gaze. Every Muslim burned by a Hindu. Every innocent citizen blown up by a suicide bomber or crushed by an onrushing, revenge-drunk tank. I know we are responsible because U.S. dollars have found their way into, and out of, every battlefield, every hospital bed, and every pocket of every terrorist in the world.

We—Black men and women in every stratum of American society—live in and are part of an eco-system of terror. We, descendants of human suffering, are living in a fine mansion at the edge of a precipice. And the ground is caving in under the weight of our wealth and privilege.

All this I saw in that column of smoke.

I don't believe that the current conflict is a war between religions, that whole cultures who believe in a magnificent afterlife are plotting to take the U.S. down with them in the glorious flames of holy war. I don't believe that our enemies are ignorant dupes fooled into slaughtering the innocent lambs of America. I don't believe that George Bush, Rudy Giuliani, or the mass arrests of dark-skinned peoples are going to protect us from the teaming millions of the dispossessed.

I believe what my father believed: that I have the same rights as the other guy. But living in a different world than my father did, this realization means that I have to make *sure* that the other guy is treated fairly. If I have running water, then *he* should have running water. If I can expect to eat when I'm hungry, then *he* should expect to eat when he's starving. If I can decide on how my body is used, then so should he. And she. That is my responsibility, *our* responsibility.

Just like when we African Americans rail against the racist institutions of the West for treating us like lesser beings, we must put ourselves to task for standing by while our economic systems decimate our neighbors.

My father realized that he was a peer, an equal. He went out in the world and struggled to make this realization a fact.

It is up to me to make sure that my dark-skinned brothers and sisters around the world have what I have. That they are not enslaved, vilified, or raped by my desire to eat cornflakes or take a drive to the shore.

The Ache in Our Souls

Some things have changed since my father's day, not everything, and not all for the better. But this is a new world for men and women of all hues and orientations. African Americans, on the whole, are wealthy by world standards. We have the luxury of schools and libraries and television sets—and fairly clean water. We have citizenship and automobiles, a place in the literature, and an almost complete domination of popular culture.

Walter Mosley

Black men and women have won Nobel prizes, Oscars, Grammys, seats in Congress, major cabinet posts in the White House, and a reserved seat on the Supreme Court. Wherever you look, there's a Black woman or man already there or on the way. America has even made a place for us in the history books. We have a month dedicated to our history.

Of course, if we studied for ten thousand years, we could never regain what we have lost: the millions murdered in the Middle Passage and the millions more clapped or born into slavery; centuries of rapine and brutality, ignorance, and work so hard that we still, centuries later, feel the aching in our souls.

African Americans were the first pure slaves of mass production, and therefore we are the first bonafide members of the modern proletariat. We have labored long and hard, while at the same time fighting for equality and recognition for what we've done and for what has been done to us.

We have forgotten Africa just as Africa has forgotten itself. We have forsaken our history under the weight of the ridicule and dominion we have experienced at the hands of the so-called

What Next

advanced cultures of America, Europe, and the Middle East. We have lost our original culture(s) in the darkness and ignorance of centuries of foreign rule.

But there are some things that we did not lose: small items, small enough to fit in a pocket, or an ear, or in the tiniest unquestioned corner of our minds. For some, it's a drumbeat. For others, it's a long tale and a good laugh at the end of the day. There's even a feeling of being separate and special and a part of a greater reality that has nothing to do with national borders or machines or vengeful deities.

For some, it's the blues—that musical home for the ironies and contradictions that Europeans strain to define in the philosophy of existentialism. For others, it's a deep religiosity that can worship heaven or hell with the same conviction and sense of wonder. For many of us, it is simply survival in a world that callously devours so many innocent children.

We Africans in America have survived for centuries, staying alive when there was no sense to life, when there was no future or past or even a moment's rest in a lifelong season of pain. We bore children and taught them that life was unfair but still worth living. We helped build a great nation, yet were denied its sweetest fruits. And still we celebrated our greatness from shadows the likes of which most other Americans have never seen.

Survival has been our hallmark. We were routed and defeated, chained and beaten down. We were murdered and robbed of our language and stories and culture. But still we saved, in our hearts, a ragged flame—something our enslavers thought they had extinguished.

This metaphorical flame is not hope or pride or even just a word. It is a guttural moan, sometimes a growl, a stubborn tenacity that wants to grow and burn brightly upon the wreckage of all that we have lost. Because if all we have left is loss, then loss will sustain us.

Looking back each year in the month of February, we study the nameless, faceless, murdered millions who suffered us into this world. While being raped and slaughtered, whipped and humiliated, they were commanded to stay silent, to abandon hope for justice. They swallowed a bitter pill, and it became a part of them.

What Next

They passed it down from generation to generation because it was all they had for a legacy. They passed it down, and now it is a part of me.

Vacant Hearts

We people of color in this nation are migrants from the dark side of America's brilliant facade, odds and ends left over after the great exertion that shaped our nation into a juggernaut of economic and militaristic perfection. And it's not just us, Black people. There are Native Americans and Chinese Americans and millions of poor white Americans who suffered and died for the railroads and steel manufactur-

What Next

ers, in wars for land and economic control. Black people were not the only victims of America's rough-and-tumble rise to hegemony. Many others have had to endure the injustices served in the name of this nation's progress. Many still do suffer.

One day, after he had been diagnosed with cancer, my father took me for a ride to downtown L.A. He was upbeat about the prognosis, which was not good, because he had lived a good life. He had made it past obstacles that he knew had hobbled and then destroyed many others. Maybe he'd come out on top again.

He took me to one of the public utility buildings where they had a good cafeteria.

"Good food cheap," my father said. He liked to feel as if he could get value out of a dollar.

After we ate, he took me to a little bridge and pointed at the skyline.

" You see that building?" he asked me.

There were a dozen buildings, but I said, " Yes."

"Koreans built that building," he said. "They came over here and lived fifteen to a room, got jobs at a McDonald's, bought the franchise, added some more, worked long hours, and then they built that building right there . "

There was pride in my father's voice for these hard working Koreans. I felt that he had given them imaginary names so that, in his private reveries, he could congratulate them personally for their success.

He waved at the skyline then and said, "Koreans built a lot of these buildings. Do you know how many of these buildings Black people have built?"

"No, Dad."

"Not one."

That was the end of the conversation, and his lesson.

My father was a proud man. He knew how hard it was for Blacks in America. He knew about the prejudicial loan policies of banking institutions, about gerrymandering and economic profiling, and about the simple-minded belief many whites held that Black people didn't have the ability to manage complex financial concepts. He knew that the cards were stacked against us, but he

What Next

didn't care. How could he?

" Walter," he used to tell me. "If you want to do as well as a white guy on the job, you have to get there half an hour earlier than him and go home half an hour later... If you want to do better, make it an hour on either side."

"But, Dad," I'd say. "That's not fair. "

"That's right," he'd reply.

Fair didn't amount to very much for my father. He had always been an underdog. That's why his victories were so sweet. He wanted Black people to have built that building, but he had nothing against the other people who did it instead. They already knew that they had to out-hustle the white man. Eighteen hours a day was like a holiday for one of them.

Today my father would be less critical of his brothers and sisters. Young African American entrepreneurs own buildings and businesses, consult with the President, and ring the opening bell on Wall Street. The World War that so changed his life has had its affect on all of us.

My father's expectations have been met, at

least to some degree, and now it's time for my generation to make demands. While my father wanted to stand side by side with the physical and economic development of white America, I want to be in spiritual harmony with the rest of the globe.

My father used the skyline of downtown L.A. to judge the advancement of Black America. I use the ruler of human suffering from Africa to Afghanistan. How can we, Black people of America, who have suffered so much under the iron heel of progress, stand back and allow people to starve and die as silently and unheralded as our own ancestors did on those slave ships so many years ago? How can we, the great defenders of liberty, allow our sweat and blood, taxes and minds to be bent toward the subjugation of the rest of the world?

Not only do we stand silently by while Kurds, Mayans, Sudanese, and South Africans die from warfare, slavery, disease, and neglect, but we also sit almost passively—knowing full well that hundreds of thousands of young Black men and women are imprisoned and institutionalized by a

What Next

police state organized around the principal of protecting the property of the rich.[1]

My father saw an empty space where a building built by Black folk should have stood. I see the same vacancy in our hearts.

---

[1] *We, you might say, live in a democracy, one of the greatest examples of liberty in the long history of the human race.* For some this may well be true. However, there's not one America but two. One of these nations is bright and beautiful and based upon democratic principles and fair play. The other is poor and suffering. In this America, medical aid is inadequate, junk food is the staple, the rent is not always forthcoming, and drugs are a means of self-medication inside a life that borders on insanity. This poor America is maintained by the police. Its denizens are familiar with nightsticks, handcuffs, and jail cells. These citizens have a different relationship with the law and with the Bill of Rights.

Four Rules

It is time for this nation to come up with a new program: a new notion of civil rights and peaceful negotiation, an international concept of harmony among the wide variety of humanity extant in the world of the twenty-first century. And who is better qualified than African Americans for this task?

We know from bitter experience what it is to be shortchanged every day, from cradle to grave.

What Next

We know the lies propagated by the media, law enforcement, and even our own government. We know that the concepts of equality and fairness are actually only commodities distributed by the institutions of capital. We know because when we went to the store for our fair share, we were told, for centuries, that there was a shortage and that we'd have to wait until there was an increase in production.

It wasn't until we shouted, "No more!" and demanded our share that things began, no matter how slowly, to change.

The world today is caught in a paroxysm of violent upheaval. In order to contain and lessen the chaotic spiral of carnage and bloodshed, we must make a commitment to peace. We must declare what it is we feel that all people in the world should expect and conversely what we all deserve.

I'm not sure that there should be one set of expectations, however. All of us have a different view of the world, but I would like to put forward the following universal ideas as the rules of fair treatment that I personally would like to live by:

- First, I cannot be free while my neighbor is wearing chains.
- Second, I cannot know happiness while others are forced to live in despair.
- Third, I cannot know health if plague and famine thrive outside my door.
- And last, but not least, I cannot expect to know peace if war rides forward under my flag and with my consent.

I believe the institution of these simple statements would halt the rampant onslaught of the haves—in whose numbers many of us are counted—against the have-nots. Murdered and enslaved children, no matter what their color or gender or faith, suffer because of our failings. Starving millions go hungry so that we may dine in comfort. Just as my father decided to believe in himself, I have decided to believe in the sanctity of others.

Stirring the Pot

The purpose of this monograph is to outline a possible approach to some global issues. It's not addressed to presidents and prime ministers but to plumbers and day laborers—and especially those African American laborers who have seen what can be achieved with their own strength and will. It's not so much a meditation on the duty of our country as a whole but on the responsibility of the individuals who make up this nation. My words here are meant to stir the pot, to add a few arguments, and to point out some of the pitfalls ignored by our television, radio, and newspaper commentators and by our political analysts. It is meant to give a glimpse of the dizzying heights of our precarious perch, imagining the unimaginable—our downfall.

A few years ago, I wrote another political monograph called *Workin' on the Chain Gang*. The intent of that slender text was to discuss the difference between capitalism and democracy while addressing what I saw as the merger of issues of race and class. When I finished that manuscript, I resisted turning it over to my publisher because I knew that I wasn't an expert in economics or politics and that there were thinkers far greater than I who had been working on these very same questions day and night for years. Who was I to tackle the major issues facing the nation when so many others were so much more articulate and erudite?

But then, as now, I remembered my father. The erudite class of his time agreed with, or at least did not argue against, Jim Crow. The leaders of his America fought for freedom in Europe while

What Next

maintaining the second-class citizenship of people of color here in the United States. It was up to my father to make his own way, to come up with his own ideas. It was up to LeRoy Mosley to negate and deny the great thinkers of his time, even though they were supposedly better educated, better trained, and better situated to understand the world's problems.

So LeRoy chose instead to strike out on his own. He would tell anybody who would listen, "If I work as hard as the man next to me, then I should get equal pay." Or, "If they take my money at the cash register, then they better hire me if I'm qualified."

Today, his arguments seem quite sensible, but back then they were radical.

I'm not saying that all educated men and women are against the struggle for world peace. There are many good and great thinkers from our Harvards and Howards alike. But a man or woman with vision cannot lead a nation that is blind. We Americans cannot be *told* what to do. We must decide for ourselves what is right.

My decision to submit *Workin' on the Chain*

Gang for publication was made because I knew that putting an argument out there that came from a mostly untutored eye was just what we needed.[2] That way, no matter how flawed or ungainly the arguments, at least I could make the statement that all of us are capable of making decisions about how our world should be run.

Many of us in Black America are thinkers. We see the contradictions and the lies. We know that our taxes fund war and slavery. We know that our nation's foreign policy is dedicated to imperialist gain, not the spread of democracy. We know that America was built on the backs of slaves.

If many everyday people in America know these things, then why can't they change the tide of world events? After all, we *are* America. President Bush *is* our proxy, not our dictator. The Congress, and even the Supreme Court, *are* answerable to us.

---

[2] I have had some education in political science. I have a BA degree in the subject and I even took a few classes in graduate school. But I have no advanced degrees nor any expertise beyond anyone else who reads the daily rags.

What Next

I wrote this book to be picked apart and dissected, not followed. I want to argue against the powerful urge for us to dominate our enemies. I want to bring about some discussion that might lead to action. I want to go beyond our fears and prejudices so that the next time I look out my window, I will know what to expect.

Part Two

Who is the Enemy?

Back before I can remember, my parents put a down payment on a house that cost $9500. They paid on their mortgage for nine-and-a-half years, and finally, the house was theirs. They then decided that we should move into a *better* neighborhood, and so we sold the house of my childhood and put that money down on a four-unit apartment building in West Los Angeles. People in the new neighborhood told us that our next-door neighbors were awful people. They

What Next

wouldn't allow the local children to walk down the driveway we shared, and they never even said "good morning" to anyone.

Remembering this admonition, I saw the neighbors from our apartment window the second day after we moved in.

"There's those awful people," I said to my father, pointing and glowering.

"How do you know there's anything wrong with them?" my father asked. "Have you spoken to them?"

"Because William and his mom said so."

"But you never talked to them yourself, now did you?" he asked me.

"No, but..."

"Then you don't know. William and his mom don't get along with the Luckfields, but that doesn't mean you won't. They might end up being your best friends if you give them the chance."

I was leery of my father's optimism, but his words turned out to be true. Whatever the conflicts were between the Luckfields and other neighbors, they had nothing to do with the great friendship that developed between our two families.

Walter Mosley

The Luckfields were white people. My father could have easily believed the worst about them. He had been dealing with condescending, cheating, humiliating white people for most of his life. But he rarely allowed himself to be the victim of the prejudices leveled against him. He gave everyone a chance to be the best person they could be.

Someone had to prove himself to be my father's enemy before he would take up arms and banners against them, before he would allow hatred and enmity to overwhelm his heart.

How do we know that someone is our enemy?

This is the first question we must answer. Who poses a threat to us? Who hates us to the degree that they are ready to do us harm? Who has contempt for our security and peace of mind?

For many people, the answer is quick and easy. It's the secret terrorist, the suicide bomber, the foreign religious radical who whips up the masses into a frenzy of hatred for America, its citizenry, and everyone who allies themselves with us.

What Next

And certainly there is some validity to this answer. When innocent American blood is shed upon our streets, when intricate conspiracies are being hatched, even as you read these words, that are aimed at disrupting, disabling, and even destroying the American way of life, then we have every right to consider these schemers our enemies.

I would push this definition even further, however. Not only are those who plot against us the enemy, but *any* assassin, *any* murderer is our enemy. We represent civilization and sophistication, while they stand for chaos. We cannot say that murder is wrong only within our borders or if committed against our citizens. If some Peruvian woman or Nigerian child is assassinated by political zealots, then that assassin is also our foe. He has to be because once we accept, condone, or excuse the wrongful death of any human being, we have negated our own right to expect justice and respect. This is why there was a presidential edict that America could not participate in the assassination of foreign leaders. If we can kill them, then they have the right to kill us.

Our enemies are the lawless dregs of a world

gone half-mad. It doesn't matter if they feel in their hearts that the crimes they commit are somehow justified. It doesn't matter if they are exonerated by their peers or religious leaders or by the moral interpretation of some government official. Murder in our realm is wrong, and anyone committing this crime is The Enemy of mankind—no exceptions allowed.

The Enemy is the same to all people, all nations. He lives here among us and over there with them. He is a man, or woman, who has denied the common morality accepted by people everywhere in the world. He is not just my enemy, but The Enemy of everyone, everywhere.

If you accept this argument, then identifying those with whom we are allied is simple and straightforward: our allies are those who do not accept murder, terrorism, and assassination as valid political discourse.

Our enemies are all persons involved in causing the deaths of others—either actively or from a consciously passive posture—for political, nationalistic, or economic ends. If, as the evidence seems to indicate, Osama bin Laden ordered the

What Next

deaths of the Americans in the tragedy of September 11th, then he is The Enemy. If our agents caused the deaths of innocent Kurds, Panamanians, or Guatemalans, then they are The Enemy. We can't have it one way and not the other. We can't say that an American life is worth more than a Sudanese life. We can't condone the violent actions of our armies and secret police if we condemn the actions of others who use violence, torture, and intimidation to obtain their ends.

We must seriously consider the possibility that we number among the ranks of The Enemy. If we can blame a group of people as a whole because their representatives use the tools of killers, then how can we exonerate ourselves if our deputies use the same methods? If we hold the German people responsible for the acts of their leaders in the 1930's and 40's, then how can we be forgiven for our actions in Cambodia, Guatemala, Vietnam, Iran, and Iraq?

Human life is sacred. We African Americans know what it is like to be treated as less than human, as inferior to our white counterparts. We know the extent of abuse that can be heaped upon people because they are not seen as part of the human race. How can we stand by as our nation, while claiming peaceful intentions, wages war on people who may not have played any part in the crimes against us?

Even if we condone military actions, we might at least claim *some* culpability for the havoc visited upon a mostly innocent population. The deaths of innocent children is not "collateral damage." The wartime death of children is the murder of innocents. And if we committ these murders, then we are also The Enemy of civilization. This is a tough argument, because it runs against the grain of present day American nationalism and fear. America has clearly identified its enemies. They are mostly the dusky skinned or Black zealots of the Islamic religion. They are almost all Arabic and, coincidentally, they sit on some of the greatest oil reserves in the world today. We believe they are a threat because their religion is different from that of most Americans, because their religion is the fastest growing faith in the world today, because their population tops the billion mark, and because many millions of this billion hate us.

What Next

That hatred, we believe, has led to terrorist attacks on us and our allies. Maybe this is true. Maybe their hatred is being expressed in religious terms. Maybe there are even those who believe in the sanctity of their violent acts against us. But the gods are put in place to protect their acolytes. If Middle Eastern religions speak out against America, I doubt that it is because our women don't cover their faces or that we practice another religion. Pressed into poverty and ruled by the whims of the almighty dollar, the cult of hatred against us is founded (I believe) in capitalism, not upon ancient texts or cultural differences. We Americans are seen as economic invaders who attempt to control everything that many people elsewhere in the world see as sacred.

The Middle Eastern populations are our neighbors, our fellow human beings. It is paramount that we make peace with them if it is at all possible. And not peace on *our* terms, but a just and equitable peace. We must treat them as my father wanted me to treat our neighbors: with an open heart and with democratic optimism.

In order to do this, we have to look beyond

the TV shows and the newspapers, past our fears and doubts. We must redefine our notion of The Enemy, taking into account the role and actions of our own political and economic systems.

The Logic of Terrorism

Ever since the WTC tragedy, some Americans have been afraid in a way they never have been before. They are afraid that death might come at them from some secret warrior, who will subvert the conventions of common warfare and go after the innocent citizen sitting at his desk or walking her baby carriage down the street. Riding a bus, eating at a restaurant, flying away to some island paradise for a well deserved holiday—any of these acts might today end up in fiery death.

Fear has made these Americans angry. *Never before*, they say, *have Americans been so badly treated and misused.* That is white male America speaking—white male America and those who identify with the myths of Christopher Columbus' "discovery," democracy, and freedom for all.

In truth, the history of America is full of the stories of fearful individuals and groups who live or who have lived with the real fear that they might be lynched, burned, beaten, castrated, bombed by American planes on American soil, and excluded from all the major arteries of wealth, influence, and dignity.[3]

Women haven't even enjoyed a century of the right to vote, and they still live in fear of sexual violence that is commonplace. America still has not apologized for its part in the genocidal institution of slavery.

This is not to deny that we are under attack from foreign agents, nor do I mean to say that

---

[3] The Tulsa Riot of 1921 is an example.

What Next

any innocent citizen deserves to live in fear because of the past deeds of his ancestors or the clandestine agents of his or her governments.

All I want to say is that we have historical equivalents to the terrorist attacks throughout American history. We have past experiences that can help us understand the dangers and the logic behind what is happening today.

America's history is littered with terrorists. Certainly Nat Turner's bid for freedom instilled terror among the white population of the South. John Brown was a terrorist. Quantrill and his Confederate guerillas were terrorists. General Sherman's march to the sea was a military exercise in terrorism. The men who bombed African American churches in the sixties were terrorists.

A modern terrorist is a single-minded being—a man or woman, sometimes even a child, who has made the decision to give up his life, or at least to give up the lives of others, to make a statement and to instill fear. We perceive these terrorists as being full of hatred, desperate, and possibly crazed. They attack innocent citizens who, to them, represent the evils that beset another group of people somewhere.[4] They decide to destroy one group of innocents to bring attention to those who have suffered but about whom no one seems to care.

For many terrorists, their sacrifice is also an act of war. For them, the war was declared long ago, but no one outside their group ever acknowledged it. Their acts of violence are, for them, striking back at the people who have been striking out at them for years.

I must add here that to understand a crime is not to forgive it. We cannot forgive murder. Murder is the ultimate offense. Still, for all our righteous indignation, we in the United States must ask, *Why do these terrorists hate us so?* We need an answer to that question. We need to know if we have been waging a clandestine war somewhere. We need to know if our actions in the Middle East and elsewhere have hurt or killed people. We have to wonder at the motivations of

---

[4] By "innocent" I mean those people who are not aware of having committed a crime and who are also unaware of any crimes being committed in their name.

What Next

the people who lead our nation because even though we, as citizens of the United States, believe that the greatest prize is freedom, we must always remember that the corporations who so inform our foreign policies value profit more than they value human life.

As the descendents of slaves, we African Americans know this is true. Certainly, Native Americans have no doubt that the urge to profit has invalidated their claim to this land. America's foreign policy has been based on ensuring profitability for the nation's business-es, not democracy for the masses. Democracy is decidedly unprofitable. A worker who can vote will seek a minimum wage and health insurance. Leaders that are answerable to their people and not to the CEOs and the CIA will work to make their people happy.

Yet, maintaining this happiness has proven too costly for our nation's oil companies and agricultural empires. Communism, organized reli-gions (possibly excluding certain elements of Christianity), and even democracy pose a danger to our rapacious capitalist interests.[5] People governed by rulers who are not answerable to international corporate empires have the power to say "no" to the endless exportation of their wealth, health, and peace of mind.

So even though it is America's obligation to condemn and fight against worldwide terrorism, we are also duty bound to find out if our actions (or inactions) have brought about a climate of desperation and violence. This means that even if the perpetrators of terrorism against the United States are evil and insane, we must ask the question: *Have we had any part in creating that evil, that insanity?*

---

[5] Notice here the separation of capitalism from democracy. These are not inherently connected concepts.

Who is at Risk?

When I was thirteen, there was a racial uprising in Los Angeles. It was called the Watts Riots. Dozens of people died as a result, and the Black part of the city went up in flames. Martial law was declared. The National Guard was called out. America was horrified.

I remember one evening during the riots, I came upon my father sitting in our living room. His head was hanging down and there was a tumbler of whisky in his hand. He was crying. At forty-nine, he had been living on his own since the age of eight. In those forty-plus years of forced emancipation, my father had seen white men killing Blacks and Blacks killing each other. He was a child of Jim Crow, herded toward colored areas of town and into the backs of busses. He had been forced to swallow his pride almost every day of his life.

"What's wrong, Dad?" I asked him.

"They're out there fighting, Walter," he said. "That's what."

"It makes you scared?"

"No."

"It makes you sad?"

"Not really."

"Then what?"

"Because," my father said, "I want to get a gun and go out there with them. I want to fight, too. I want to go get a gun and go out there and tear down all this shit they put on me all these years."

The thought of my father out there in the streets with all the angry men and women I'd seen on TV was deeply frightening. I didn't want

What Next

him to go. I didn't want him to get killed. I *needed* my father.

" Are you going to go?" I asked him.

This question seemed to hurt him all the more. Now I look back and realize that he felt challenged by me. When he saw the men and women fighting, he felt that they had found the courage he could never muster, and that I, too, was questioning his bravery. The rioters weren't afraid of the white policemen or of American racist oppression. They were willing to stand up against the centuries of abuse. And there he sat, crying in his drink.

"No," he said at last. "I can't."

My silent relief was lost on my father. He started talking to me as if I were questioning his decision.

"It's not a *real* war, Walter. It's just a bunch'a people tearing down their own stores and their own neighborhood. Most of the people getting killed are Black people, and they're outnumbered. They're right to be mad, and they *should* fight. But those stores are *theirs*. Once they burn down, they're not coming back. It's the wrong way, honey," he said. "I want to be out there with them, but they're wrong."

I must have asked my father if the business-es weren't owned by white people because he said, "It doesn't matter. Property changes hands all the time. The man on top today retires or dies, and somebody else takes his place tomorrow. But if it's all burned down, then there's nothing left to own."

I stood next to my father and put my hand on his shoulder. I hope today that my touch gave him some comfort. He lived a long-suffering life so that I could tell his stories. I hope he knew that his words were not wasted.

The years have passed, my father is dead, and the Black population has mostly fled South Central L.A. for the outer suburbs and other parts of town. Chicanos have taken our place in more ways than one. And I'm looking out of my Greenwich Village apartment window, thinking about my father's tears.

Who is most at risk from the terrorist attacks on America and Israel? From what I hear on the streets of New York, most people think that it's us: Americans of all races. School teachers, pub-

What Next

lishers, taxi cab drivers, philanthropists, and drug store clerks all seem to be talking about the danger the Arab world poses to the well being and freedom of American citizens.

"There's a billion Muslims in the world," I've been told more than twice.

"So?" I reply. "There's almost a billion people in India and over a billion Chinese."

"The Shiites and Sunnis teach hatred for the United States and Europe. There are a million terrorists waiting to blow up our schools and theaters and department stores."

"How can you know that?" I ask. "Don't you believe that what most people want is to live in peace with full stomachs and healthy bodies? Are the Muslim Arabs or other Muslims that different from you and me?"

"They're going to wage World War III against us and Israel, and they outnumber us four to one."

"How," I ask, "are they going to wage this war? With what planes or weapons? With what navy will they approach our shores?"

"With a million suicide bombers," I'm told. "They're in hiding across America, just waiting for orders to blow up our cities."

The argument is interminable. Ignorance, coupled with fear, fuels America's racist opinions of the Middle East. It is just like the riots of 1965. White America was afraid that Black America would overflow the ghettos and rain down destruction on them, while my father sat crying realizing that we, Black people were defeating ourselves by destroying our own resources and turning the nation against us.

And my father was not alone. Most Black people sat out the riots in their homes, protecting their families and hoping that the National Guard would bring order with a minimum of violence. They knew that we were going to be the big losers in the riots.

The Middle East would be the big losers in a global war. They have no ally that will stand up to the one remaining super-power—the United States. They don't have the mechanisms of destruction to make us afraid of an all-out attack. If anyone is at risk in this war of terrorism, it is the Arab nations, and maybe Israel. Numbers of bodies mean nothing when compared to multi-ton bombs or even nuclear capability.

What Next

All of the bakers, plumbers, restaurant owners, housewives, and day laborers of the Middle East are living under the shadow of American rage. Osama bin Laden couldn't mobilize the Islamic world against the West because they know, like my father knew, that you don't wage a war that you can't win.

The Wages of Hate

W hen my father was sitting there in our darkened living room in the 1960's wishing that he could go out and join the melee, I became aware of something that took me many years to work out. My father was far beyond simple outrage. He wanted *revenge* for all of those years that he was mistreated and for all the millions upon millions of Black people who had been murdered and robbed, raped and silenced. He wanted to go out into the streets and yell and fire his gun into the void of his oppression. Did he hate? Most definitely. Should the people he hated have been afraid of him? Without a doubt.

LeRoy Mosley was the victim of a system of racism that had ruined his people for six, eight, ten, and more generations. He was the inheritor of that bitter pill. He was the survivor who found himself with the possibility of finally getting revenge. *"Burn, Baby, Burn!"* was the catchphrase of the riotous Sixties. Those words were screaming in my father's mind.

He, and millions of other Black men and women, hated white America for the five days of the Watts Riots—for those five days and for generations before and after them. His smoldering wrath was justified by his experience. He never once questioned his own culpability for the racist institutions and their adherents. America was afraid of my father. More than ever, America wanted the part of his mind that held this deep grudge to disappear. And if my father, and the millions who felt like him, could not drop their hatred, America wanted them to disappear.

This is only natural. No one wants someone who hates them to be anywhere near even the periphery of their territory. Their mere presence poses a threat. All the years before the Watts riots, white people could ignore their history and their crimes. *"That was a long time ago,"* we were taught in school. *"But Lincoln freed the slaves."* Now the grandchildren and the great grandchildren of those slaves were cutting up, acting out hatred that went all the way back through centuries of abuse.

Once again, my father's seminal story rears its head in my memories. This time it's white America saying, *"They couldn't be at war with me. I never did anything to those people."* But white America had to wake up, if just a little, and realize that dark America was writhing in an endless nightmare.

Seeing my father so wretched over his decision to stay at home during the riots made me feel very insecure. After all, my mother was a white woman. At least that's how I saw her when I was thirteen. She had very white skin and Caucasian features. Her family had lived in Europe for many generations. But my mother is also Jewish. In America in 1965 she was a white woman. In

What Next

Germany and most of Europe, at least before 1945, she was a race apart. Racial classifications are finally just cultural attitudes. I don't think of my mother in racial terms today, but in those deeply disturbing times, she was a white woman who made up half of my world.

The Luckfields next door and many of the people my father worked with were white. My father wasn't duplicitous, either consciously or unconsciously. His friends were his friends before and after the riots. He would have died to protect my mother from harm, and he would never have hurt her. He didn't bad-talk whites because of their race. He never excused himself because a white superior criticized him. If the criticism was wrong, then he'd say so. If the criticism came from racism, he boiled. But he was always rational and responsible.

My father would never become his enemy to make a point.

So, why did he want to go out with his gun and a Molotov cocktail during the summer of '65? Why did his heart race with a dark pride when he saw his fellow Black Americans wreaking havoc?

Of course, I've already answered this question. The hatred lived *inside* my father. It lives still in the hearts of so many Black people in the United States today. It is part of the legacy of slavery, racism, and Jim Crow. It is something that my father and most Black Americans have learned to live with. He never fired his gun or burned a building. He never allowed himself to commit the crimes that were committed against him. Most of us haven't. We understand that the choice is between building and tearing down.

There is a long discussion issuing from that painful realization, but that is not the topic of this book. The only purpose that my father's muted rage has here is to help us try and understand the rage that men and women around the world feel toward America today—especially the Muslim population of the Middle East.

The similarities are undeniable: African Americans vis-a-vis a group of people who feel intense political and economic pressures from an external culture, people who are pushed to adhere to standards that make them feel like outcasts in their own culture, their own skins. We see these people on CNN or on the covers of our

What Next

magazines and newspapers. They are enraged, dark-skinned people burning effigies and flags, marching and loudly denouncing the capitalist imperialists—*us*. From Pakistan to Saudi Arabia, they rage. For decades, they say, America has interfered with their religion, their money, and their rulers. Sometimes, we deny the claims. Sometimes, we give reasons for supporting this king or that despot. Sometimes, we simply run away. Often, we get involved with covert military actions. But lately, we've been preparing for all-out war.

This sort of international politics presents a deep quandary for African Americans. I realized that when I saw Colin Powell being burned in effigy on the streets of Pakistan. They didn't think of him as a Black man, a "Negro." They certainly didn't see him as a son of Africa. He was an American pressing American policies on a people who are sick of our policies and our representatives.

They don't identify with my father, but I see some of him in their rage. I imagine ten thousand Pakistanis for every one that stands in protest. I imagine these men and women sitting in their

Walter Mosley

houses feeling impotent and seeing America as their enemy. I see them wanting a world that is forever denied them. They are living in poverty in a nation surrounded by enemies. They are a people who want to realize their dreams in a world that vies to control their every thought.

They hate me. I wish that this hatred would disappear in just the same way that white America felt about my father's hatred. I find myself oddly in the position that whites found themselves with regard to my father's generation. Yet here I am, feeling no enmity toward a people who hate me. They celebrate when I am attacked and damaged. They pray for my downfall.

White America recoiled at the images of African American hatred. They ran to the suburbs. They elected Richard Nixon. They complained of their innocence. And in ignorance of their own history, they believed in that innocence.

White America has had centuries to hone the myth of American incorruptibility. It's hard to fault the full-faced, happy Americans who believe in the Constitution and the right of every

What Next

American to vote, who believe in democracy and freedom of religion and a free marketplace. Traveling in the limited circles of middle-class America, anyone would be hard-pressed to deny the utopian majesty of our nation. We have clean water and automobiles, televisions in every home, and policemen who patrol the streets. We have firemen and elected representatives and free schools and vast quantities of food, clothing, medical aids, alcohol, and tobacco.

The America that exists for the middle class is beautiful.[6] But there are places that my father and I have both seen that deny this American Eden: poor America, working-class America, and the gray area between those two suffering masses. The millions of men and women who travel the revolving door between the ghetto and prison.

---

[6] There are many interpretations of class. If you lived among people who made ten dollars a week while you made a hundred, you might be seen by your neighbors as being rich. My particular definition of the class of an individual is based on that individual's relation to labor. A person who, having lost their job, has to get another job within a few weeks to avoid being evicted, or at least threatened with eviction, is a working-class person. A man or woman who, upon losing a job, has a grace period of six months or more is a member of the middle class.

The children who go to bed hungry. The elderly who are shunted into systems of maintenance but not care. The mentally ill, the sick, and the undereducated, who make up a large portion of this paradise. And those suffering masses are the lucky ones. At least they have the chance of being associated with the American Dream.

There's the magic of wealth in America, but what about the rest of the world?

Afghanistan was the poorest nation in the world before the WTC attack. And while AIDS decimates Africa, we Americans only have to look at our recent history to see the carnage that we've created on a worldwide scale—the bombing of Cambodia and the senseless, endless war on the Vietnamese people; the slaughtering of thousands in Guatemala; and the invasion of Panama. We have embargos against the leaders of nations who never suffer want, leaving only the innocent populations to endure our punishments.

Our freedom and comfort comes at a great cost for our own citizens and people around the world. Middle-class white America and its aspi-

What Next

rants have been blissfully ignorant of this situation.

African Americans are not so lucky.

Can the Victims of History Become the Heroes of the Future?

Black America has never had the luxury of the self-deception of the middle-class. As my father said when I was eight, *"I didn't know that I was an American."* The systematic victimization of my father and his ancestors put African Americans in a unique critical position. We can identify with the prey of U.S. foreign policies because we have also been that prey. We

What Next

can understand the rage of people who have been bamboozled by American rhetoric on democracy because we have been lied to about freedom and carry a similar rage in our own hearts. We know all about profiling and displacement and being ruled over by people who do not have our best interests at heart. We know about being colonized, body and soul, by powers that have never recognized our bright spirits and keen minds.

Before continuing to describe these essential characteristics of African American perception, let me say that I believe most African Americans today see themselves as Americans. We don't want to leave this country or abandon its beautiful notions of individual freedom and dignity. It's just that we know laws and philosophies don't work when they aren't applied equally and with great commitment.

And we know that American economics is often at odds with our democratic ideals.

The almighty dollar doesn't recognize the value of one commodity over another. One hundred dollars of human labor is equal to one hundred dollars in silver. That's a fact. And if a man is worth a hundred dollars for his labor, but the company can realize a hundred and one dollars from a bag of manure, then the manure is more valuable than the man. If there is some notion or person who defies this system of value, then that person or that notion is worthless to that system.

Freedom? Worthless.

Dignity? Rubbish.

God? Insignificant.

Laughter? Well, maybe if there's a comedian doing a concert or a sitcom making fun of men being raped in prison—maybe that might earn a few bucks. Maybe a minstrel singing his heart out, Black skin under a coat of black paint, can generate some worth. But what is he worth? Only what I am compelled to pay.

Poverty has honed our ability to appreciate freedom. Oppression has whetted our appetite for justice. The ignorance of our slave masters' heirs has focused our attention on fair play down to the ultra-fine details.

We, African Americans, are probably the most qualified of all Americans to pass judgment on our nation's notion of fair play. We know when the cards are stacked against someone. We know when the "fix" has been put into the game. And because we have seen so much suffering, we are the first to want to give succor and relieve pain.

But how can we relieve the world's pain? By bringing about a cessation of the relentless pressure being applied by U. S.-supported kings and oil companies. The world does not need to be answerable to our Congress or our president. The people of the world need to find their own way toward capitalism and democracy. They need to practice their own religions and their own customs.[7] They need to eat and have medical care and education. Many Americans need these things, too.

These requirements may sound easy to attain to many white readers. But Black Americans know what it's like to have to demand the sim-

---

[7] In making this particular claim I realize that I am opening a Pandora's box of the kinds of sexism practiced in cultures not our own. This is a serious and heart-breaking problem that cannot be pushed aside to simplify our commitment to world peace. But as we must recognize the inequities in foreign cultures, we must also critique our own systems of prejudice. What of the millions in prison, the ill, the mentally ill, the homeless, and the aged here in the United States?

plest dignities and still go on unheard. We know what it is like to have to look down when a white woman walks by or to worry about a child being lynched or beaten for feeling his oats. We know what it's like to get the leftovers and still have to pay full price. We know what it's like to live in a world where our images are either absent or reviled.

It wasn't that long ago that we were kept from voting booths by armed men. It wasn't that long ago that a Black face would be unheard of in Congress. Still today, we are greatly underrepresented. We still feel restraints that other Americans cannot imagine.

At some other time and place, these declarations would be grievances. And at another time I will return to the similarities between our industrial-prison complex and the institution of slavery. I will come back to the deep psychological damage done to the entire American spirit, both Black and white (and brown and yellow and red), by our leaders and their constituents who have turned their backs on the philosophical implications of a nation built upon the twin pillars of plunder and slavery. But right now, I am appeal-

What Next

ing to Black America. I'm asking us to stand up and enter the dialogue about our nation's war on the Middle East before we find ourselves deeply enmeshed in a logic of violence and murder that will put us on an equal par with the slavemasters of old.

Our Silence

I t has struck me that the political voices of Black America have been comparatively quiet since the events of September 11th. We still talk among ourselves, of course. And then there ' s Condaleeza Rice and Colin Powell—those two powerhouses of political clout are working hard to bring the situation to a conclusion. But I don't feel that they represent the full spectrum of African American thought.

Many people might say, and I'm sure they think, that the silence of Black America is a tacit

What Next

agreement with U. S. international policies. One might also believe that, Black Americans and white Americans have attained parity, a oneness in their stance against their enemies. I don't think so.

No. Our silence is a part of our conditioning.

Our ancestors were stripped of all things physical when they came to this country. They were left with nothing, not even a bronze ring or a string bracelet, to separate them from any other beast of burden. Clothes, once they were given, were, on the whole, rags. Our only property was our ability to think, our sense of self, because even our bodies were not ours to dispose of as we saw fit. We were treated as mindless property, and thus our minds were at least partially formed around the notion of our situation.

What were we to think? White skin was master's skin. Black skin was less than. Freedom was the province of another race. Slavery was our kin. Liberation was our destiny, but what a small prize that is, really. My freedom, or even my people's freedom, is only a single step toward justice when there's a whole world straining to be free.

My father and I heard about the assassination of Martin Luther King, Jr., at the same moment. The news came in over the radio. Shot down in Memphis. The civil rights leader was dead. As the hours went by, news unfolded about people rioting and crying, people praying, and people being stunned. The nation entered into a period of mourning. One of the greatest leaders this country had ever known was murdered for having a dream.

My period of bereavement was cut short because of something my father said.

"It's that Vietnam," he told me. "That's what got him killed."

"What are you talking about?" I said. I was sixteen by then and often angered by my father's irrational claims.

"As long as he wanted to march around and talk about Black people getting some freedom, they let him crow," LeRoy said. "But let him try and grab at their power, and they laid him low. "

That kind of talk continued for a while. Basically, my father's argument was that as long as Black people stayed in the ghetto and

What Next

remained comparatively nonviolent, the authorities would allow protest and even, to some degree, change. But once we stood above our own complaints and began to question the authority of the children of our slavemasters, we were bound to be put back in our "place."

I don't know if my father's words were accurate. King's assassination is still clouded in mystery and controversy. I don't know if my father was right, but I do know that he wasn't alone in his way of thinking. I do know that many thousands, maybe even millions, of African Americans believe that there is an invisible barrier between us and the true reins of power in this country. And if by strength of character or circumstance one of us crosses that line, that someone will be stopped. Either he or she will be killed, discredited or bought off, but they will almost certainly be stopped.

Is this fear valid? I'm not quite sure. And it doesn't matter even if it is true, or somewhat true, or if it has been true at some other time in our history. It may well be that the hegemony in America is against African American participation in politics of a global nature, but that doesn't mean that we should hold back or maintain the silence that we were forced to live inside of for so many centuries. We have attained all the rights and responsibilities of American citizens, and we should exercise those rights to the fullest.

Silence is the worst enemy of freedom. We cannot be quiet. Even if our voices cause conflict and consternation, even if some things we say are unpopular, even if there is danger involved, we have to remember our responsibilities. We are the bright sons and daughters of America's tragic beginning. We are at least part of the answer to making it right.

Part Three

Making It Right

How do we African Americans stand against the chauvinist attitudes of this nation, its politics and economics, while understanding the hatred the rest of the world feels against us, and still condemn the uses of terrorism? The precipice we stand upon is gravelly and unsure. The only thing I know for certain is that standing still will send us, sooner or later, plummeting to our doom.

I hesitate to give an answer, but not because I'm afraid of being wrong. I'm sure that there will be many flaws and chinks in any argument made for a world peace in which we common citizens can participate. The steps I suggest may all be wrong, but at least they will provide a stand that we can reject. And in rejecting one notion, others may come forth.

About the goal there is no question: unequivocal world peace and security, freedom from starvation, and respect for the sovereignty of all nations.

In a gesture toward this goal, I'd like to put forward the thought that there are two sides to the problem, so there must be at least two sides to the answer. On one side, we have the Islamic world and its antipathy toward the West, especially the United States and its ally, Israel.[8] The

---

[8] Israel has to be considered here because it represents a microcosm of the larger conflict between theWest and the Middle East. The domination of the Palestinian people can almost be seen as a metaphor for the way many Arabs feel that they are being treated by theWest. There is no solution that can overlook the problem in Palestine.

What Next

Islamic world is typified, maybe even stereo-typed, by religion and race. It is represented as almost primitive compared to the seeming sophistication of the West. This representation is, of course, inaccurate.

On the other side is the United States of America, which is generally perceived purely on the basis of its economic appetites. This view is also an oversimplification.

Certainly, the sophistication and intellect of the Islamic and Arabic world are beyond ques-tion. Without them, the West might never have known its own Plato. The mathematics, language, astronomy, and literature of the world have been deeply impacted by Arabian and Islamic schol-ars, artists, and philosophers. Pictures of ranting mobs or criminal gunmen do not define the whole culture of these groups any more than an episode of "COPS" tells us about America, crime, or the predilections of Black and poor white American youths.

Americans believe, or at least they *think* they believe, in freedom and democracy. They extol the virtues of freedom of religion and the con-cept of one person, one vote. Americans believe in self-determination and the inalienable rights of the individual. Most Americans believe that our history and our political culture is based upon these concepts. Yet, we are fooled by the rhetoric of our national heritage and, in that hoodwinked condition, we make false assumptions about the face we show to the world.

The forces that drive us forward do not rise up from any notion of equality. Instead, our political system, which is greased and maintained by large amounts of cash, finds its greatest constituency in the dollars that maintain the power of our two largest influence corporations: the Democratic and the Republican parties. Money—not democratic ideals, the Bill of Rights, or humanitarian beliefs—makes up our foreign policies. The hunger for cheap oil and the subsequent investment in corrupt and despotic rulers comprise our true face to the world.

Because of our actions, much of the rest of the world experiences the U.S. as a pillager-nation. Our corporations, backed by our armies, swoop down upon the so-called Third World, culling cultures for all they are worth. But in vilifying the capitalist shell of our foreign policies, the victims also vilify the American people. This makes sense. Don't we always malign our enemies? It's just human nature.

But as I said above, we Americans don't necessarily believe in the practices of our corporate structures. Many of us feel the plundering effects of big business in our own work lives, bank accounts, energy bills, and certainly at the hospital. Today, many Americans have lost vast quantities of cash betting on the hollow promise of the stock market. College funds and retirement accounts have been depleted and lost while the captains of capital remain well-heeled and unaffected.

Freedom is a negative commodity in our daily lives—something that is a side effect of the dollar—not an inalienable right of our idealistic Constitution.[9] We in the United States experience

---

[9] It's all good and well to say that I have the right of free speech, but what good is that without access to the media that dollars control? It's fine to say that I have the freedom to pursue happiness, but how can I pursue something that I can't afford? How can I be happy suffering under the agitation of debt brought about by the ever-increasing weight of the credit that keeps our banks in business?

the plundering of big business just as our African, Arabian, and South American neighbors do.

Still, most Americans, just like my father, say, "Hey, I didn't do anything to you! I'm not a rich man. I'm just a poor schlub trying to make my rent, pay my children's dental bills, earn my daily loaf, and maybe, if I'm lucky, still have enough left over to buy some beer. "

A strange balance comes into view if we look at the conflict in this logic. On one side, there are the peoples of the so-called Third World being manipulated and impoverished. On the other side, there is the common American citizen, doing better on the whole, but by no means rich, not even secure, considering the current job market and volatile economy. In the middle, there is international capitalism, which makes its home base in the United States and Europe. And the wealth is concentrated in the center, while the sides play this antagonistic balancing act.

I'm sure this situation is recognizable to African Americans. It's an act we've been playing to packed houses ourselves since 1863. Ever since the Great Emancipation, there have been

What Next

poor whites on one side and poorer Blacks on the other, hating each other for something that neither one of them started.

My father realized in France that his enemies were those who had fooled him into believing that he wasn't an American with all of the rights of an American. His personal war was to attain that freedom. Black America's collective war is to assure that same freedom on a worldwide basis. What we have to do as a whole is expose the real culprits of worldwide strife and strike back at them. Blowing up mountains in Afghanistan is all good and well, but we can't expect that to stem the tide of hatred. You can't expect starving and disenfranchised peoples to be daunted by the threat of violence when they live under the violence orchestrated by U. S. corporations' puppets every day. That trick didn't work on Black America, and it won't work elsewhere.

No, threats won't work and violence comes back unless you commit the ultimate crime. And even then, the victims will have survivors.

No, we cannot threaten or bully our neighbors. What we must do is seek to limit the rapaciousness of our pillaging corporations. We must separate our political notions from our economic goals, and we must strive to emulate the spirit of our political and philosophical beliefs.

African Americans know these goals and how to fight for them better than anyone else in the world. We have, drawing upon the ideas of great thinkers like my father, moved a whole nation to begin to understand the problems inherent in a government that, though based on the ideals of democracy, uses the forced and coerced labor of its own people—and others—to realize its goals.

We have been only partly successful because we have almost exclusively looked at the problems of this nation.[10] Now we see that a whole world is suffering. This knowledge, I believe, can lead us to a deep understanding that will ultimately lead to a real international peace accord.

---

[10] We do have exceptions. Not all American activists have been insular in their political actions. From Frederick Douglass to Marcus Garvey to Martin Luther King, Jr. to Malcolm X, we have had leaders who sought answers on an international level.

Steps Toward a World Peace

The most effective tool we Americans have to help us work toward world peace is our conviction to create harmony in the world. No strategy, no bomb, no amount of cash alone will bring us and our neighbors into alignment. If the American people today were to shift their fearful and angry hearts toward a desire for peace, the world would change quickly and wonderfully into the paradise we all desire.[11] No FBI wiretaps or nuclear detector devices will protect us from determined enemies.

We are the richest and most powerful country in the history of the world. Our will and culture have charged the atmosphere and the dialogues of the world, for good and for bad. If we give in to fear or support the domination of the world's impoverished billions by our corporations, then strife, war, and death are inescapable. And in that conflagration, we too shall be consumed.

But if we take the stand that our enemy is the secret assassin—no matter what his or her philosophy, nationality, religion, or race may be—then the gentler side of human nature will be allowed to inform our ragged and brutalized world.

But, you say, America is living in fear. The terrorists have succeeded in bringing us into the dialogue on their terms. Instead of rising above their fears, Americans are buying canned food and thinking

---

[11] Very few people enjoy the full potentials of our intellectual and technological wealth. Creating peace and well-being for others will also increase our own bounty.

What Next

of relocating to Australia.

Peace for our leaders has, for too long, been making other countries agree with our primary concerns (which, paradoxically, have been dictated by terrorism). To expect Americans to turn around and work for peace and harmony seems almost impossible. And for most Americans, maybe it is. But African Americans know how to tackle the impossible. My father's lessons were all about following one's own beliefs, regardless of the enemy, his numbers, or his monumental arrogance.

The truth of your beliefs is a powerful weapon against fear-mongering leaders. The fragility of the so-called Third World, the fact that most people in the rest of the world are simple laborers who want the bare essentials of life, the truth that we are more likely to support dictators and terrorists than truly democratic leaders—all of these facts are our weapons against fear.

My father's decision was a simple one. All by himself he moved to an American frontier, California. Without a battle cry or a political organization, he settled in Los Angeles and made his own personal stand against racism. At first he thought that he was alone in this battle, but after a while he saw people around him and even people in the news who were saying the same words, taking the same stands. Even just one voice of support is succor against a thousand enemies. My father and his thousands spoke louder than the millions who opposed or ignored them.

That is what we must do. We have to make our will for peace and justice be heard over the fearful cries being orchestrated by our nation's popular media and leaders.[12] In the following pages, I will put forth some ideas that might have some value in helping us reach this end.

---

[12] When the Democrats blamed the leader of their competitors for overlooking vital information that might have thwarted Osama bin Laden's machinations, the Republican vice president proclaimed that terrorist activity was unavoidable. It wasn't a question of if but when they would strike at the U.S. This obvious manipulation of the fear of the people went almost undetected. This wasn't an act of leadership, but simply "good business."

The Organization

Our federal government and the nation's big business are closely connected on ideological and economic levels. This means that the interests of democracy and justice often take a back seat to the expediencies of profit. Even our armies rank second in power to the corporate infrastructures. Influence begins and ends with the ambitions, necessities, and strategies of corporate control of the worldwide systems of production. Our politicians' unquestioning commitment to this hierarchy makes us (the United States) the most formidable force in almost all aspects of human endeavor on a global scale.

This hierarchy could not have the power it wields without the unfailing support of our legislators and the executive branch. So when we turn to our senators and our president, we must be aware that their concerns cannot be fully in line with the order formed by pure democracy. Health care, sovereignty, and even dignity and reserve of judgment do not lend themselves to the needs of our economic machines. And so, if we trust in the spirit of the law, our ultimate American dreams will always be stymied by the underlying requirements of the organization of wealth.

Because of this political predicament, I do not believe we can change the will of our government without first coming together in smaller organizations that are external to the recognized political systems. In other words, grassroots organizing is the *only* route for real democracy in our lives.

Capital controls the skies and seas and the shifting plates of the great continents. Its magnitude dwarfs most nations and all religions. Money

What Next

changing hands and deeds tied to land are the real gauges of power in our world. Wealth is the judge of worth, even in spiritual terms.

If I hadn't been raised by my father, I would be daunted by this reality. But instead, I am heartened by the fact that his situation was so much more difficult than ours. He was completely alone, or at least he thought he was. All by himself he decided to change his relationship to the monolith of American racism.

I have it easier. I *know* that there are thousands, maybe millions, of African Americans out there who agree with my quest for world peace. Beyond Black America, there are millions more who hunger for peace, whose purpose is to transcend the consumerist doctrines that have overrun our lives. Yet, we are isolated from each other by the structure of our so-called political parties, by the overwhelming amount of information gushing out of the media, by the lies and silences perpetrated to maintain the interests of big business, and by the all-too-human trait of concentrating on the immediacy of our lives while ignoring the experiences of the larger world. The anguished masses of Africa, the Middle East, and elsewhere are so removed from our sensual experience that we somehow manage to live guilt-free lives, even though we have intellectual awareness of suffering around the globe.

This incongruity echoes another contradiction manifest in our daily lives. On the one hand, our problems stem from the fact that we do not think on a large enough scale to deal with the problems facing the world today. On the other hand, our one apparent avenue for large-scale political action—the federal government and most of those whom we elect to its offices—is working to maintain the brutal system of corporate pillagers.

Damned if I do, my father used to say, *and damned if I don't.* And then he would laugh.

It is in the laugh that lies the hope.

Forget the large scale. Forget the proxies. What we need is each other and the recognition between us all that peace is within our reach. To these ends, I am going to discuss a variety of obstacles to a new peace movement and suggest pedestrian responses designed to move mountains. I will talk about the media, local politics, Marcus Garvey, funding, and the philosophi-

What Next

cal underpinnings of a possible African American-led peace movement.

Mastering the Media

Our greatest resource and greatest enemy in this effort is the media. The only way we can keep up with world events is by watching, reading, and listening to our news broadcasters and journalists. But of course, the news is not objective. The media sometimes warps and misrepresents and, because it is a business, often exaggerates the news to make us want to pay attention, therefore meeting its primary demand: obtaining the largest possible audience for advertisers.

What Next

This is not to say that the news doesn't get out or that journalists are rapacious capitalists who practice fiction instead of reporting the facts. CNN, MSNBC, and other 24-hour TV outlets provide a great deal of the information we need to decipher a complex world. C-SPAN is extraordinarily objective in presenting the world. And of course, there's the Public Broadcasting System, National Public Radio, and the Pacifica Radio Network, three outstanding national organizations that speak to listeners and viewers from a less economically encumbered point of view.

If only we could spend the necessary hours pouring over the various shows and publications, contrasting and comparing their information, we might find that the world we believe in is not the world we live in.

Talk radio is another outlet that at least questions the logic of our leaders' decisions and the ramifications of world events. Then there's the Internet. Online, we can follow a key word through millions of permutations and associations. The World Wide Web can hand anyone almost as much information as the president can put his hands on. But the truth is well hidden, and truth seeking is not a valued job in our nation today.

The problem is that there's too much information. Americans put in more hours at work than any other laborers in the industrialized world. We don't have the time to spend three, four, five hours a day ingesting and deciphering world events. We can't research the history of every revolution, terrorist organization, and corporate interest. It's hard enough just to read the front page of the newspaper or manage to get the full eight-and-a-half minutes of radio's headline news.

And it is just these headlines and info-bites that are the most co-opted by advertising dollars. The most frightening, the most urgent, the most bloody news appears where we get the majority of our information. THE DOCTOR OF DEATH, BIN LADEN'S HIT MEN, BUSH KNEW. We typically read these headlines with their few explanatory words, and we're off to work or to bed, or turn on some sit-com that will soothe our worried hearts.

What is the answer? Certainly, the media can say that it only puts out what the public wants to see—sex, violence, mass murder, and the signs

What Next

that might lead to foreknowledge of some new threat from foreign radicals. Deep analyses, long reports, or incrimination of the American political and economic systems are not sought-after formats, whether or not they are appropriate.

"If the people won't listen," the news programmer asks, "then how can we tell them?" In truth, they can't. If there aren't enough hours in the day, how can I know what's important? This may seem an impossible obstacle to overcome, but I think there is an answer. It depends on our connecting with a small group of intimates who are willing to share the burden of knowledge. Alone, there are few who can follow the news in its entirety. But if there was a small group that met together in a den, a restaurant, or even on the phone or online once every two weeks or so, they would be able to share the information that they'd gathered. We have time for book groups, prayer groups, bridge groups, bowling leagues. Why not have a night set aside to try and grasp the meaning of world events?

Imagine it. A night where five or six or seven acquaintances get together simply to share information that they've gathered. One man can make it his concern to follow the war on terrorism, its emphases, and its goals. A woman can follow claims and indictments originating from the Middle East. At the same time, a young student can read the financial pages of the *Times* or the *Post*. He or she can tell the group what's going on in the stock market and with the Congressional appropriations.

Another approach might be to break up the world into geographical sections and have each news group member be responsible for one or more of these areas.

Imagine the conversation. All the aspects of national and world events can be brought together over a period of time among this small group. Each member can share information with other individuals who are also overwhelmed by the glut of the Information Age.

It is up to each of us to gather and use the information that is presented to us from so many different sources. If seven people spend one hour a day each reading in one area, that means the group can spend a full work day studying the issues that face us.

What Next

Human beings mastered their environment eons ago by working together. Unity is still one of our finest tools.

I realize that this is a small step, and maybe it seems hard to understand how a few people sitting down and talking about news they've read over the past week or so will make a difference. But the truth is that knowledge is the only real power to which we have access. One by one, we're weak, but together we can increase each other's authority and awareness to the point where we will be able to make decisions that might lead to change. School taught us how to study; now we can use those skills to defend ourselves against all of those who would practice the art of the secret killer.

And when we are looking for information, let's not stop at the *borders of western imagination.*[13] Major newspapers and national news magazines are fine, but there are European publications and also South American, African, and Asian media

---

[13] This term I borrow from Clyde Taylor, professor of English and Africana Studies at New York University.

that will give, if not less biased, at least different- ly biased views of the world of which we are so much a part. Many of these publications are in English, but it wouldn't hurt to have one or two members of each news study group who are liter- ate in another language.

The Internet can also be useful in allowing direct contact with people in Saudi Arabia, Palestine, and Pakistan. Through online transla- tors and search engines, we can personally begin to understand how the Islamic world describes itself. Maybe everything we hear won't be hopeful or any more truthful than what we hear from our own media, but at least we will begin to understand the desires of the people in the Islamic and Arabic world today. Any commu- nication is better than utter darkness.

As much as I want to indict the media, it's really the structure of the world that stymies awareness. Just as the capitalist cannot change the rules of competition and the means and mode of production, the journalist cannot control the avenues of the media nor the complexity of the news. We must overcome these convoluted conundrums by coming together to share our

What Next

investigations, trying to tease out the illusive key to our deliverance.

Political Action

Once we have begun to bring the world into view by sharing information and working together, we can begin to make changes through political actions. Through our studies, we can identify public officials, personalities, and places that support our growing ideas and attitudes. We will need to nourish those that seek peace. We will need to come together in creating points of political pressure that will force larger government entities to pay attention to our demands.

What Next

These points of political pressure can be alder-men, city council members, judges, U.S. Representatives, or mayors—political representa-tives with whom we can meet and talk, who live and work on the same level that we do. These are peo-ple who are answerable to us, who can open up the books and explain their actions—or inactions.

Marcus Garvey, the early twentieth-century Pan-African leader, wanted to gain political and nationalist hegemony by creating a Black nation. My distrust of large political systems in our current economic culture makes me leery of such a grand political move. I prefer going in the direction of taking over neighborhoods and small communities where the quest for peace and global justice is the predominant attitude. A mayor representing a town of twenty to fifty thou-sand residents is more trustworthy than a senator or president who requires endless quantities of capital to maintain his complex goals.

We need to think on a larger scale within the limits of what we can see, who we can touch, and in terms of the true American dialogue: democra-cy.

For those of us who don't live in a community that lends itself to these ideas, there are various alternatives. One radical move would be to relocate to a community that agrees with the goal of peace. Another thought, just as extreme, is to run for a public office that will allow you to speak out for peace. If enough small study groups come together, they might even have their own private election, choosing a spokesperson who will address venues open to them.

And if all else is unworkable, there are still the old-fashioned methods of political action.

We should protest every unwarranted act of war—every embargo, every refusal to help enhance the quality of life in disease-ridden, famine-plagued nations. These protests include marches, letters to the editor, letters to Congressional representatives, and just plain talking on the street or at work or on the bus at night. We should protest political murders wherever they happen. Protest should be our language and our creed.

We, and our Islamic counterparts, should strategically boycott American and international corporations that are not fully committed to world peace as a part of their economic plans. No more fruit companies or oil concerns or their minions deciding on international policies, governmental actions, or suppressing political activities in other countries.

The only threat to a corporation is the bottom line. A corporation runs on its profit margin; everything else is just a means to an end. Life and death are alien concepts to the company store because a business has no awareness, no heart. If New York City were blown off the map tomorrow, business would continue. If your daughter or son were to die by the hand of some terrorist whose own child was murdered by the plundering of one of our companies, there would be no vice president coming over to apologize for his part in your sorrow. But you'd better believe there would be someone there to placate you if it meant getting your dollars back into their coffers.

Our dollars are being spent on companies that use slave labor, that support dictatorial regimes, that try to regulate any cultural aspect that gets in the way of business, like public health, education, or any other form of social welfare. This act of commerce is why we are responsible for what happens in the far-flung corners of the globe. We don't *vote* for worldwide oppression. *We pay for it.*

Funding

Money is always the high hurdle. At some point along the line we're going to have to put together funds to pay for language translators, speakers' travel fees, ads, Internet space, bumper stickers, and maybe even food for starving peoples.

Whoever manages this money and the type of supervision under which it will be released will be faced with the stickiest problems—that, and deciding on how the money is to be spent.

The answers to these questions are beyond my expertise and the limits of this monograph. But I do have an idea on how to raise funds.

Most Americans have a jelly jar or coffee can somewhere that's about halfway filled with pennies, nickels, dimes, and quarters. There are billions of dollars laying fallow at any moment in dark closets and bottom drawers. Once we have set up a mechanism for dealing with this money, we can, with our children, begin to collect this vast national treasure to fund a world peace movement.

Change for change. It means many things. It might be a catchphrase for an entire movement.

Ideas

Sovereignty. The most important issue in the world today is sovereignty. So-called Third World nations are struggling against disease, poverty, cultural incursions, and the American government's maintenance of its corporations' business interests.

People in the streets here in America are saying that we cannot allow radical Islamic extremists to rule in their own countries, even when their own people may want that type of governance.

Our government and our corporations try to influence political organizations and even the electoral processes in foreign nations by applying liberal amounts of cash in the right places. The desires of the people hardly seem to matter.

If we don't respect the independence of our sister nations, we will get their ire in return.

It is necessary for us to limit our pillager-corporations in their dealings with foreign nations. We can do this by boycotting goods produced by these companies, but we can also legislate their activities. If we can levy an embargo against a country that offends us, why can't we withdraw support of American-based corporations that support foreign despots?

This is also true for our own branches of international activity. The World Bank, the CIA, the State Department, our ambassadors, and our armies should all be there to make this world a better place. We already have the largest slice of the world's pie. We already have the biggest guns and the brightest skies. We already have TVs and cars and paved roads that cover hundreds of thousands of miles. We have Hollywood and Cape Canaveral and Wall Street. Now it's

What Next

time for us to let our neighbors have something, too.

And not just our white European brothers. Africa should flourish, and South American wannabes should not be armed with American rifles. North Koreans should not be starving by the millions.

How can we do all of this? Well, it's most likely that we can't. But at least we should devour a little less of the world's resources. We could limit the trillionaire corporations. We could invest in solar power and make mass transportation a priority. We could assist the millions who go in and out of prisons and the mentally ill men and women who have no home but the streets. We could increase the wealth of our minds and live a simpler life.

I'm not saying that we should give up our armies or our national defense. We should stay strong because the world today is a volatile place. But our nation is the cause of much of this volatility. Our rapacious appetites—fed by ever-growing conglomerates that hide behind the myth of globalization—impoverish and starve a good part of the rest of the world. In order to serve our endless need for fresh meat, bananas, and petroleum, our government and our corporations undercut and blindside whoever is weaker.

And we must remember: Survival of the fittest is the slogan for capitalism, while justice and fair play are the watchwords of democracy.

Revenge. Let's not forget the reason we exact our pound of flesh from our enemies. It's not for justice that we bomb and burn and slaughter. We do it for revenge or out of fear. These primitive responses are natural and older in their nature than our very species. Because of this we have to respect the motive, but at the same time we need to question it.

I spoke to a young man who told me that we had to bomb Afghanistan because the Taliban were deeply involved with Osama bin Laden and therefore were, at least in part, guilty of the suicide bombing of the World Trade Center. Revenge, in his reckoning, was fair and just. I referred him to President Clinton's admission of our own involvement, through the CIA, with the decades-long assault upon Native Mayans in Guatemala, an assault that may have caused

What Next

the deaths of two hundred thousand people.

"Does this mean," I asked the young man, "that these Mayans have the right to bomb and burn targets across the United States?"

Should American vacationers in Vietnam sleep with one eye open, fearing reprisals from the relatives of the millions who died there because of our aggression? Should the Kurds or the Iranians, the innocent Iraqi citizens, or the survivors of Nagasaki and Hiroshima be forgiven if they decide to slaughter every American they lay eyes on? What about the civilians who died in Dresden or the innocent bystanders who became collateral damage in Panama?

We must have it either one way or the other. Our house is definitely made of glass. We, as a nation, are not innocent. We have killed. We have slaughtered. We have filled mass graves and moved on without a word or apology or sign of lament. And so, if we say that revenge is an accepted behavior, then we make ourselves the target of the revenge of our victims.

I don't mean that we shouldn't protect ourselves or that we don't have the right to use our power defensively. But we should be aware of the consequences of these actions. Reactions to them may bring us beyond the threshold of safety.

Our Role in Creating *The Enemy*. On the surface the attack on the WTC seems simple to understand. We were beset by Islamic extremists who wish to practice Jihad upon the West.[14] Certainly there is a grain of truth to this thought. After all, Osama bin Laden made these claims and lived by them.

For most Americans, however, this is the end of the investigation of the causes of terrorist activities against us. But what if there is another reason? What if the bombing in Oklahoma City is related, in its spirit, to the actions of Middle Eastern radicals? What if the source of the violence is one group, no matter where from, that feels disenfranchised by the powers that be? What if any group who feels silenced by the larger financial corporations and by the influence corporations (i.e., Democrats and Republicans) is a potential terrorist organization? A terrorist

---

[14] The term Jihad is greatly misinterpreted in the West. Though it may, in some aspects, have to do with holy war, it is also a concept of internal struggle and self-betterment.

What Next

might come from any quarter. After all, we have seen Irish, Israeli, and South African terrorists in the last half-century.

It might be that the cause of terrorism has more to do with us than we are willing to believe. It is possible that terrorism can arise from any corner of the world or our own country. If this is true, a war on any group will ultimately be use-less because the practice will rise from some other quarter, as long as we don't pay attention to our part in the problem.

Of course, some terrorism comes from natural conflicts that arise within our culture. The issue of abortion comes to mind. It is likely that we will have to be alert to self-styled enemies of our laws and beliefs, but we must also question our actions in the world. The more we try to limit the economic freedom and the political organization of domestic groups and other countries (espe-cially in the so-called Third World), the more we open ourselves to the possibility of violent response.

Cynicism. A powerful obstacle to world peace is American cynicism. Many, many times I have been at a dinner table or walking down the street where people are saying, in essence, "The sky is falling! The sky is falling!" They worry about anthrax attacks in the mail, they see anti-radiation pills given out freely, they fear suicide bombers on every corner. It's all too much, they cry. The world is coming to an end!

Not hardly.

There may be more terrorist attacks on American soil. There may be another round of anthrax scares. I can't be sure about that, but I can promise you that there will be earthquakes and fires and plane crashes. There will be murders and rapes and robberies. There will be unemployment and cancer and boating accidents. There will be sexually transmitted diseases, premature baldness, and Alzheimer's disease. I can promise you that each and every one of us will die one day and that most will leave loved ones bereft and crying.

But for all my promises, I don't think that you should despair. Life in America in the twenty-first century is a good life for most of the people reading these words. We have libraries, access to antibiotics, freedom of speech, and maybe even someone to love.

What Next

It makes no sense to cringe in some corner because some tiny fragment of the sky might fall one day. It makes no sense to live in fear when life is so good.   It certainly won't help to become a pessimist.

What the world needs now is hope for a better tomorrow. That's where our labor and our love belong.

Again, I say this to Black America. We know how to live in a world where a violent end is a good possibility. We know when we walk out on the street that there's a chance that we might not only be profiled but actually arrested, tried, and convicted for something we did not do. This doesn't take away our ability to dance or sing or make love. This doesn't keep us from planning for a brighter tomorrow.

We must raise our voices and object to the gutless cynicism and pessimism that so many Americans hold onto like a security blanket. Get up and get out and work for a better day! Don't sit in the dark waiting for some imaginary terrorist. Find out if there are any children starving somewhere and try to get a crumb across the border to them. Find out who in your own neighborhood is virtually illiterate and go read to them. Tell a joke. Do something that reflects the fortune that you have lived with for so long that you have begun to take it for granted.

Every day that we wake up is a good day. Every breath that we take is filled with hope for a better day. Every word that we speak is a chance to change what is bad into something good. We aren't slaves, concentration camp victims, starving Koreans, or even inmates forced to live in an overcrowded prison. We are free women and men living in the richest and most powerful country in the history of the world. This nation is at least a *potential* democracy. We need to wake up from this walking nightmare and realize that the sun is shining and that the fields are indeed ripe with grain.

Two Suggestions

The entrance of the United States into the global struggle, which includes terrorism, has caused some permanent changes in our national psyche. One of these changes is the dawning realization that we are hated by so many people in the world at large. The second change has been slower to come, but it has to do with the technology we have helped to develop and the need for decentralization of our historic power structures.

Both of these issues, to one degree or another, can be addressed by African American thought and experience.

The first issue is very straightforward. We African Americans have been living with people who have hated and despised us since the day we were first taken from our homelands and carted off to the plantation. The White Citizens Council, the Ku Klux Klan, the American Nazi Party, the Supreme Court, and many others have taken venomous swipes at our inherent rights. We've been kept out of neighborhoods, voting booths, country clubs, and educational institutions because of our skin. No one person had to do something wrong in order for us all to be vilified and hated.

But all that time, we only wanted to be free members of the American society. You could hate us all you want, but just let us have freedom and equality!

African Americans know how to live with hatred. We've been stopped for walking in the wrong neighborhood, lynched for looking up the wrong skirt. We never liked the mistreatment, but we never gave up the dream, either. We know in

What Next

our hearts that all people are equal and essentially good. We hold that truth to our breasts and move ahead without hesitation. Let's keep that up during this crisis. Our backs are strong enough to bear up under the weight of the hate people have for us. And let's critique the faint-hearted other Americans who feel they can't bear living in a world where they are despised.

Without giving in to cynicism, we must face the fact that weapons of medium to mass destruction are, at least at the moment, near at hand to many different and dissatisfied people. Because of this, we might want to consider changing how we do business. Even now, our president and vice president try not to be in the same place at the same time. That's only sensible, seeing that we need to have a leader who is in the know.

It reminds me of another story my father told me. This one was actually a retelling.

My father's favorite novel was *The Godfather* by Mario Puzo. He liked the old don who stood up for his values and his sense of justice, despite the old world religiosity that spawned him and the new world prejudices that disdained him.

Walter Mosley

" Walter," my dad asked me after I had read the novel at his suggestion. "You read the part where the cops shut the numbers rackets down after Michael shot McKlusky?"

"Uh-huh," I replied ineloquently.

"But they couldn't shut down the Black folks because they couldn't catch'em. They didn't know where to look."

My father loved the fact that Black people knew how to become scarce when they needed to be, that we knew how to conduct business in the worst of times.

We live in a country that answers to a central government that is permanently anchored in Washington, D.C. One well-placed bomb could damage all three branches of our government to a devastating degree. Why not separate the branches then? Send the Senate to Montana, the House of Representatives to Miami, the Supreme Court to San Francisco, and other federal courts to Mississippi or Iowa? Why do we need a central power source accessible to lobbyists and bombers?

I say this partially because it seems obvious.

What Next

The Information Age has made proximity an unnecessary burden. We can be in continual and direct contact over vast distances and safe in our mutual isolation. The other reason I bring up this point is that we, ordinary everyday people, can think about the problems that loom over us. We can organize and reorganize. We can put ourselves in the true position of greatness by making a world where life is sensible, sacred, and sure of its moral atmosphere.

Conclusion

The problems that the world faces today cannot be solved by superior strength alone. We Americans must use our hearts if we want to face the hatred confronting us. And we must be able to look critically at our own actions and motivations if we want to understand our enemies.

This kind of empathy comes hard for most Americans because we have such a muzzy understanding of our own history. Our past has always been depicted by images of upstanding white men conquering nature and "heathen

What Next

From the so-called primitive red man to Adolf Hitler, we've always seen ourselves as standing strong against the enemies of freedom and modernity. Sometimes our cause has been just, and often it has not. But never has an American campaign been so complex. Today we need more than John Wayne and the Winchester rifle. Today, we need the subtle compassion of Black America, with its fine-honed attention to the etiquette of liberation.

Our collective freedom, fellow Americans, depends on our ability to defend the rights of others. All Americans should understand this concept, but I fear that it might only be Black America that has the historical perspective to move this notion from an idea into action. We, of all Americans, know what it's like to lose everything in order to come into alignment with the American Dream. Not only do we have a moral stake in protecting the innocent victims of the present war against terrorism, but we stand to profit spiritually from the process of working for peace.

Walter Mosley

Some of the greatest ambassadors representing American culture in the twentieth century have been Black people. Louis Armstrong, Muhammad Ali, Martin Luther King, Jr., Josephine Baker, and many others have gone abroad, with or without our government's blessings, to show the world the beauty they have found here. They were men and women of peace. For over a century, African Americans have represented America's culture and its high moral ideals, not its penchant for economic domination. While the American government was selling arms to the world, we were delivering jazz. While U. S. presidents waged war on foreign ideals, African Americans spoke of peace.

Today is just a continuation of that history. We have to get out there and work for peace. We have to reject the fear mongers and the profiteers. Certainly, we have to protect America. Certainly, we have to arrest and monitor those who have made it their express desire to harm our nation. But we must also remember that there will be no defense if the whole world hates us.

We must remember, the only true defense is peace.

Post Script

Reading over this last section I can see how one might be unhappy with the strength of my *solutions* in the face the staggering problems we have to contend with today. I can hear people saying that we must have decisive and strong responses to these problems. Some will say that we need stronger armies and greater covert intelligence gathering (even at the expense of our rights). Others will call for abandonment of our allies and our commitment to the Constitution and the Bill of Rights.

My small groups and articulation of some subtleties may seem to be a weak broth.

This critique, I fear, has some validity. But it is my opinion that much of what I have said here is not a part of the general dialogue; that many African Americans have not worked through our own culpabilities and responsibilities in world discourse. You have to be able to walk before you can run. You have to be able to read before you can understand the road signs you come upon.

This said, I will share one resource that has helped me to understand the world as it relates to our dark sisters and brothers. TransAfrica Forum, with its president Danny Glover and its executive director, Bill Fletcher, is one organization that seeks to bring to light the pain and difficulty that faces the African diaspora and beyond. I believe that contact with TransAfrica Forum (202-223-1960 or www.transafricaforum.org),

What Next

will lead many to a fuller understanding of what is at stake and what we can do about it.

As I have said before: the answers will come from all of us. We will be a wave of clear reason and justice in a world that lost its way.